Pigeons in the Great War

A Complete History of the Carrier-
Pigeon Service during the Great
War, 1914 to 1918

BY

Lt.-Col. A. H. OSMAN.

London:
"The "Racing Pigeon" Publishing Co., Ltd.,
19, Doughty Street, London, W.C.1.

The Naval & Military Press

Published by

The Naval & Military Press Ltd

Unit 5 Riverside, Brambleside
Bellbrook Industrial Estate
Uckfield, East Sussex
TN22 1QQ England

Tel: +44 (0)1825 749494

www.naval-military-press.com
www.nmarchive.com

Printed and bound by CPI Group (UK) Ltd, Croydon, CR0 4YY

CONTENTS.

———

ILLUSTRATIONS.

Lieut.-Col. A. H. Osman.—His thumb mark and pass.

INTRODUCTION.

On the 17th August, 1928, I received a letter from my old chief under whom I last served on the Headquarter's Staff at Horse Guards, saying that "during the war he scarcely or properly appreciated all that pigeons did for the cause," adding, "Now I know better."

Neither the general public, nor fanciers themselves, I fear, have ever appreciated the scope of the carrier-pigeon service during the great war.

It has taken me a good many years to decide to compile some details that may assist in the removal of any doubt that the carrier-pigeon service on all fronts was a valuable one.

Towards the end of the war 150 British mobile lofts, with complete equipment, were in active service on the French and Italian fronts. This will give some little idea of the extent and usefulness of the service.

In addition to mobile lofts, we had stationary or fixed lofts, and in England we had a series of lofts for intelligence work at stations along our coast line from Newcastle-on-Tyne to Hastings.

I received much sympathy and help in the arduous work undertaken in connection with the carrier-pigeon service from Col. H. de Watteville, Captain Ashmead Bartlett and General Shaw. To these officers I feel it my duty to offer thanks for the consideration at all times shown me.

From the original pigeon service, evolved to help trawlers not fitted with wireless communication to send reports of observations and findings to the Admiralty, was eventually evolved the three important carrier-pigeon services of the Army, Air Force and Navy.

I shall first of all deal with the formation of the war committee that helped to allay the suspense and alarm that rested on all keepers of pigeons when war broke out. In later chapters I shall relate some few of the services performed by birds and men in the different spheres of action.

Throughout the duration of the war, fanciers loyally helped in every possible means in their power; and to the credit of our sport be it said every pigeon supplied to the British Army at the front or for home defence was given free of cost to the country.

Quite 100,000 pigeons passed through my hands for active service, and not a single bird for any of the services was ever enlisted unless certain it was sound and capable for the work it was likely to be called upon to perform. It was impossible to say when any bird might be the last resource of a platoon, or airman brought down on the ocean.

From the inception of the service I impressed upon the authorities that to be a success the pigeons at their lofts must be in the hands of experts, and every man enlisted had to pass a strict examination as to his capabilities as a fancier and trainer.

Men may be taught to shoot, fire guns or drill, but, as Darwin says in the "Origin of Species," "It takes years to become a successful pigeon fancier."

It was by the enlistment and co-operation of successful pigeon fanciers that the usefulness of the carrier-pigeon service was attained, and to officers and men who assisted in this good work I take this opportunity of tendering my sincere thanks.

I must also put on record the debt owing to the "News of the World," whose columns were of the greatest service during the war, both for the purpose of obtaining men for enlistment and the collection of birds for the service, also for the publicity from time to time we were able to give of brave deeds performed by our birds on active service on the few occasions that the Press Censor permitted.

CHAPTER I

IMMEDIATELY after war was declared a ban was placed on the removal of pigeons or their transit by rail. Railways were given notice that they must not carry pigeons for flight or from owner to owner.

Loyal fanciers who felt the call to arms and wished to enlist were thus prevented from disposing of their pigeons.

Following this stoppage of transit, police visits were made to fanciers' lofts and all confined prisoner pigeons condemned, the owner was compelled to clip their wings to prevent their flight, or give them their freedom. Many valuable birds were lost through this regulation.

The War Office then had the good sense to consult me on the subject of regulations and other matters associated with the sport, and I at once got in touch with Mr. Percy Illingworth and Mr. Basil Thompson, of the C.I.D., who had charge of secret service regulations and was responsible for the edict stopping the transit of pigeons by rail.

Having fully discussed the matter with Mr. Illingworth and Mr. Basil Thompson, I was authorised to draw up and issue a special label permitting the transit of pigeons when sold or being sent to shows, and it was on my suggestion that the N.H.U. should, if they desired, take over this business in its entirety.

Major W. H. Osman.

Capt. E. Burden.

Lieut. John H. Jacques.

Capt. C. E. L. Bryant.

Soon after this it was decided to form a Voluntary Pigeon War Committee consisting of Messrs. Handel Booth, Godfrey Isaacs, representing wireless, the President of the N.H.U., its Secretary, Mr. J. T. Hincks, Mr. A. W. Skinner and myself.

This Committee, in the first place, drew up a useful illustrated brochure divided in chapters and illustrated with photographs of "The Carrier," "The Dragoon," "The Show Homer" and "The Racing Pigeon."

The object in giving these illustrations was to help the police to discriminate between the different varieties of pigeons that could and could not be used as messenger carriers.

Shortly after this , under the Defence of the Realm Regulations, Regulation 21 was incorporated as follows :—

No person shall keep or have in his possession or carry or liberate or bring into the United Kingdom any carrier or homing pigeons, unless he has obtained from the chief officer of police of the district a permit for the purpose, and if any person without lawful authority contravenes the provisions of this regulation he shall be guilty of an offence against these regulations, and the chief officer of police or any officer of customs and excise may, if he considers it necessary or expedient to do so, cause any pigeons kept or brought into the United Kingdom in contravention of this regulation to be liberated, detained or destroyed, or, in the case of pigeons brought into the United Kingdom, to be immediately returned in the ship in which they came.

Any person found in possession of or found carrying or liberating any carrier pigeons shall, if

9

so required by any naval or military officer or by any sailor or soldier engaged on sentry patrol or other similar duty, or by any officer of police, produce his permit, and if he fails to do so, may be arrested.

Following is a copy of the permit referred to in the regulations :—

DEFENCE OF THE REALM REGULATIONS.
Regulation 21.

Number J181

PERMIT TO KEEP CARRIER OR HOMING PIGEONS.

To All whom it may concern.

By Virtue of the Powers vested in me under the provisions of Regulation 21 of the Defence of the Realm Regulations, I hereby grant permission to the Person named below to be in possession of Carrier or Homing Pigeons, not exceeding one hundred and fifty in number, to be kept (in open loft) at "Apsley House," Cambridge Park, Leytonstone.

NAME OF HOLDER.

A. H. Osman,

Christian Name, Alfred

Registered Postal Address, as above.

S. Allan Sykes,
(Superintendent).

Hackney Police Station.

A. Osman,
Signature of Holder.

Date, 5th June, 1915.

Germans loading birds on to aeroplane.

Motor mobile loft.

The holder of this Permit is not authorised thereby to liberate any carrier or homing pigeon away from its own loft. In order to carry any carrier or homing pigeon, it is necessary to obtain the prescribed official label from the Police. The holder should carefully note the provisions of the Regulation, which is printed on the other side.

This permit may be revoked at any time.

Whilst exhibitions of pigeons were permitted to be carried out, for the time being all training and racing of pigeons was stopped.

Lord Kitchener was then head of the War Office. He was a stern disciplinarian, and I learned at a later date he had the strongest objection to pigeons on account of the danger of their use for inter-communication by spies, who infested our country at the outbreak of war.

Lord Kitchener was right in the strong lines taken at these early stages, but he did not foresee the great possibility that pigeons might offer, nor was he apparently aware of the preparations the Germans had made long before the war to have an efficient mobile pigeon service.

As an instance of this a German doctor, shortly before the war, paid visits to various lofts in England, making full enquiries and taking copious notes relative to the breeding of pigeons, and also making full enquiries as to whether our War Office was in touch with fanciers for the purpose of their use.

Moreover, a full-blooded German started a loft adjacent to 19, Doughty Street, London, to which he trained pigeons. These pigeons were all destroyed during the early stages of the war, and the "gentleman," who represented himself to be a "Dane," has not been seen or heard of since his arrest. So I was not worried by such a neighbour very long after the war commenced.

Police permits numbering 500,000 were issued during the war to pigeon keepers, North Staffordshire and Lancashire applying for the greatest number.

When the difficulty of obtaining corn and food for pigeons arose, with the help of the Controller I was able to obtain supplies for all breeders of racing pigeons who undertook to breed birds for the forces.

CHAPTER II

HISTORICAL.

On the 16th November, 1870, the following notice was posted at the General Post Office, London :—

OPEN LETTERS for PARIS.

Transmission of by Carrier Pigeons.

THE Director-General of the French Post Office has informed this Department that a special Despatch, by means of Carrier Pigeons, of correspondence addressed to Paris has been established at Tours, and that such Despatch may be made use of for brief letters, or notes, originating in the United Kingdom, and forwarded by post to Tours

Persons desirous of availing themselves of this mode of transmission must observe the following conditions:—

Every letter must be posted open, that is, without any cover or envelope, and without any seal, and it must be registered

No letter must consist of more than twenty words, including the address and the signature of the sender. but the name of the addressee, the place of his abode, and the name of the sender—although composed of more than one word—will each be counted as one word only

No figures must be used, the number of the house of the addressee must be given in words

Combined words joined together by hyphens or apostrophes will be counted according to the number of words making up the combined word

The letters must be written entirely in French, in clear, intelligible language They must relate solely to private affairs, and no political allusion or reference to the War will be permitted.

The charge for these letters is five-pence for every word, and this charge must be prepaid, in addition to the postage of sixpence for a single registered letter addressed to France

The Director-General of the French Post Office, in notifying this arrangement, has stated that his office cannot guarantee the safe delivery of this correspondence, and will not be in any way responsible for it.

By Command of the Postmaster-General.

GENERAL POST OFFICE,
    16th November, 1870.

Printed for Her Majesty's Stationery Office, by W. P. Griffith, Prujean Square, Old Bailey, London, E.C.

This was the outcome of arrangements to despatch messages to the besieged citizens of Paris during the siege of Paris, 1870-1871.

M. M. Dagron, who was the photographer on the balloon "Niepcè," that left Paris on November 12th, 1870, subsequently published a thrilling account of his adventures.

Two balloons left Paris at the same time—"Le Niepcè" and the "Daguerre." The latter was shot down in sight of the passengers on the "Niepcè," which escaped by jettisoning part of its baggage and rising to a greater altitude. Subsequently, landing inside the enemy lines, the party, by the help of French peasants, obtained disguises and escaped after the loss of the second balloon.

After many adventures en route through the enemy lines, they arrived at Tours with their pigeons on November 21st.

Owing to the large number of despatches received, the messages were photographed very small in order that as many as possible could be carried by the same pigeon. The photographs were on little thin films of collodium and each film would hold 2,500 messages.

The small picture of one of these original collodium pigeon despatches is in my possession and is reproduced of exact size. This collodium pigeon despatch was sent into Paris from Tours during the siege. It contains 200 letters of 2,182 words; its weight was $\frac{1}{2}$ a gram, and the postage paid on this message was 1,000 francs, equal to £40.

Collodium Film—Actual size.

14

The Dundee Life-Saver.—Flew 22 miles in 22 minutes. The message carried saved two airmen's lives.

"Wun Hi." The only survivor.
The only survivor of two seaplanes; although shot in eye, safely delivered its last message.

Letters from England were forwarded to Tours from London in special envelopes, of which a reproduction of one of the originals is given, and although this pigeon service was carried out under most adverse conditions during the winter months, having started in October, 1870, and continued for some months during the winter of 1870-1871, many thousands of messages were carried over the Prussian lines and safely delivered in Paris, no doubt giving the besieged citizens relief and hope.

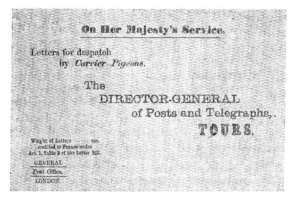

On Her Majesty's Service.

Letters for despatch
by *Carrier Pigeons.*

The
DIRECTOR-GENERAL
of Posts and Telegraphs,

TOURS.

Weight of Letters
credited to France under
Art. 1, Table 2 of the Letter Bill.
GENERAL
Post Office.
LONDON

On February 3rd, 1871, a single bird arrived in Paris carrying 40,000 messages.

When the pigeons arrived in Paris with the small collodium messages the films were enlarged by being put into a sort of magic lantern, which threw the image on to a screen from which its messages were copied down in manuscript and transmitted to their destination.

The sport of breeding and training long-distance pigeons in France was not as popular as it is to-day and consequently few pigeons were available for the service.

In a lecture on the subject by Capt. G. G. Aston, of the Royal Marine Artillery, which I attended, he gave the following table of figures of birds tossed during the Paris siege and those that homed safely with the messages :—

Month.			Tossed.	Arrived.
September and October			105	22
November	...	...	83	17
December	...		49	12
January	...		43	3
February	...		22	3
			—	—
Total			302	57
			—	—

From these figures it will be seen that the percentage was a very small one, little more than 25 per cent., but it must be borne in mind that it was an emergency service; untrained birds were suddenly called upon to do the work during winter months.

The result was very different during the recent war, when 99 per cent. of the messages sent were safely delivered, winter or summer, rain or shine, showing the advantage of using selected birds of pedigree, trained and in the hands of experts.

In consequence of the services rendered by pigeons in the manner mentioned, European nations gave some little attention to the development of the pigeon service.

In the Boer War they rendered some useful work by carrying despatches and plans out of Ladysmith, and as the war proceeded it was decided to make same little use of them by erecting small lofts. After the conclusion of the Boer War some birds were shipped to Nigeria for the purpose of establishing inter-communication between the South and North. By this means, if the blacks caused trouble at one station, pigeon messages could be sent to the other and relief sent that could attack the revolutionists in the rear.

The advent and improvement of wireless has been the means of doing away with the use of pigeons for many services, but for espionage, scout service work and many important duties pigeons will never be replaced.

A pigeon silently flies through the air; there is no wave that indicates its use, nothing that indicates its point of departure or destination.

CHAPTER III

WHEN the War Committee referred to in Chapter I was formed I expressed the opinion that it might be called upon to function in connection with the use of pigeons as messengers at no distant date. Hostilities had not been in progress many months before this view materialised, and the Admiralty decided that pigeons might render useful services.

One of the earliest steps taken by the enemy was to lay mines in the North Sea to endanger our merchant shipping as well as naval work. It became necessary to organise a service of trawlers for mine sweeping, for which service our fishing fleet of trawlers bravely responded. Many of these trawlers, when they put to sea, had no means of reporting progress or communicating with their base.

I felt I could not accept the position of lieutenant in the R.N.V.R. offered to organise this service, but Mr. Romer, having at that time just retired from professional work and having relations in the Navy, was offered and accepted the post, with my son as assistant.

My son had previously, on several occasions, offered himself for enlistment for active service, but on account

A camouflaged mobile loft somewhere in France.

German loft, captured and exhibited at the Zoo.

A mobile loft, somewhere in France, camouflaged.
The birds found their homes anywhere.

of defective eyesight and varicocele, was rejected. He was therefore glad of some opportunity of service in the war.

To be of service the owners of lofts to be employed were chosen from those living as near the coast as possible. The service was placed under the direction of Col. Dixon, a most efficient officer and organiser, with Lieut. Romer as expert pigeon officer.

Having obtained a complete list of suitable lofts, letters were addressed to the owners asking their co-operation and the use of their birds. In no single case was a refusal met with.

Although the service was started in October, 1914, when the birds were badly in moult, I at once put every bird in my loft in training, as my home loft was only 30 miles from the coast.

I had 60 birds at that time. Over 30 had flown 400 and 500 miles, as my loft had just got to the top of its form in 1914, and although these birds were trained day after day throughout the winter of 1914 and from then on throughout the war, my losses were comparatively nil.

The distance birds had to fly for the Naval pigeon service was from 70 to 150 miles. By giving them constant liberty in all weathers, they covered these distances winter and summer with regularity. As an example, on three successive weeks I had one pigeon home from the middle of the North Sea bringing dispatches and she was one of those subsequently awarded a certificate of merit for her work in this service.

Some of these messages were of a thrilling nature, but the receivers were not allowed to divulge their contents. In some cases they were in code, and of course it was then impossible to decipher them.

I remember one of the despatches my birds carried from the North Sea described an attack made upon the mine-sweeping fleet by a Zeppelin, the first time a Zeppelin ever left Germany to attack us.

The skipper of the trawler described what had taken place and that the mine sweepers remained uninjured and were able to continue their work after the Zeppelin had tried to destroy them.

Evidently at this stage the aim of the Zeppelin crew was not very accurate at objects on the sea.

When it is remembered the rough passage these birds had, sometimes sparsely fed, and that they were often handled by brawny sailormen who had been given but few lessons in fastening messages on the birds before use, it is surprising how consistently and well they homed.

A credit to their breeding and to the owners who, like myself, did not hesitate to offer their very best birds for the service.

On one occasion I lost three of my most valuable birds and never heard of them again. I felt sure, if given their liberty at any distance or almost in any weather, these birds would have homed. It was not until after the conclusion of the war that I heard my good pigeon 1100 and the other two lost with him must have been sunk by a torpedo by the enemy, as the trawler, with all hands on board as well as the pigeons, after putting to sea, was never heard of again.

Some of the skippers of these trawlers got very fond of the pigeons and treated them as friends, but there was sometimes a comic side to the messages sent.

One skipper sent a message: "All well; having beef pudding for dinner."

As owners had to take all messages received to the nearest post office, this message would pass through to the Lords of the Admiralty and then back to the base to which this particular trawler was attached.

For the duration of the war the skipper was known as "Beef Puddings."

One of the most fortunate and meritorious performances in the naval service was that of the red chequer cock known as "Crisp, V.C."

When the skipper of the trawler "Nelson" was attacked by a "U" boat, he defied the Germans and fought his ship to the last. Lying mortally wounded on the deck, he scribbled a hasty message which was sent off by this pigeon. This was his last act before he died. The pigeon carried it to a vessel in the vicinity and help was sent to the gallant trawler crew. It arrived in time to save the rest of them from death. Skipper Crisp was awarded the posthumous V.C.

The naval pigeon service was continued throughout the duration of the war, but in some cases was gradually superseded as the trawlers became fitted with wireless.

Fanciers in recent years since the war have no doubt much to thank this branch of the service for, as it introduced racing pigeons to a class of men who are now often able to render them first aid if driven to sea. Many birds in distress take refuge for the night on the friendly mast or deck of a trawler and being brought to land on completion of the cruise in the morning, they are liberated with a message accounting for their absence.

These good offices should invariably be immediately acknowledged.

They are frequently the act of men who learned to have a kindly feeling for their winged messengers during the war, but who, nevertheless, deserve the best thanks of fanciers for saving their favourites from a watery grave.

Some 500 to 600 owners were awarded certificates for the meritorious performances of the birds they lent for naval purposes. This list was published in the "Racing Pigeon," May 31st, 1919, ring numbers of the birds and names of owners being set out, but the particular meritorious performances are not given. An illustration of the certificate appears facing this page.

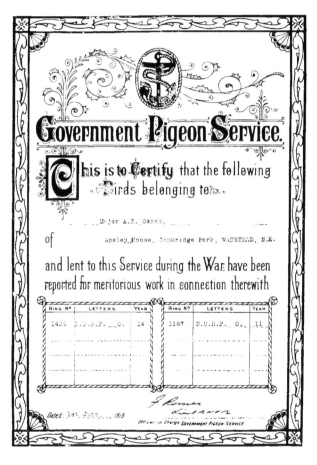

Government Pigeon Service.

This is to **C**ertify that the following Birds belonging to

Major A.H. Osman,

of   Apsley House, Cambridge Park, WANSTEAD, N.E.

and lent to this Service during the War have been reported for meritorious work in connection therewith

Ring Nº	Letters	Year		Ring Nº	Letters	Year
1425	N.U.R.P. O.	14		1187	N.U.R.P. O,	11

Dated 1st June 1919

J. Romer
Lieut Col?
Officer in Charge Government Pigeon Service

CHAPTER IV

In the early stages of the war there was no co-ordination between the Navy and Army. Each Command took such steps in organising as was deemed expedient, and no doubt for a time there was overlapping.

Hardly had we started to establish the Naval pigeon service referred to in Chapter III, than I received an urgent message from the War Office to meet Col. Maud. This officer discussed with me the situation with regard to pigeons, and stated that a Home Defence pigeon service was expeditiously needed for the whole of the Eastern coast of England, consulting me as to the best means of its establishment.

I considered the best means of meeting the request was to form a volunteer service without requisitioning lofts, and that by this means fanciers capable of conditioning their birds and keeping them fit if called upon in emergency would be at the disposal of the Command. If necessary, should the enemy effect a landing, these owners could at once be put in uniform.

Col. Maud thought the scheme an excellent one and begged me to undertake the work of its immediate organisation, with the rank of Captain.

Outside the Higher Command few of the public are aware of the fear that was entertained of a serious invasion and the steps taken to meet such an emergency.

I pointed out to Colonel Maud that my paper, "The Racing Pigeon," might be the means of obtaining volunteers and birds for the Service, and the only conditions upon which I could undertake the work was that of a honorary rank—without pay—and I was appointed to organise and command the first Carrier-Pigeon Service in the British Army on these terms. From the day I accepted a commission until the completion of the war I worked on these terms.

Whilst in the midst of selecting sites for home defence depots and arranging details, a call came from France to enlist 60 men for active service in the Carrier-Pigeon Service. It was impossible to deal with this matter as well as proceed with the organisation we had in hand. These 60 men were therefore enlisted at Leeds by the N.H.U., but at a later date, when the home defence service was established and in working order, all other men and Carrier-Pigeon Service requirements for the Army were dealt with by the Carrier-Pigeon Service at Headquarters, Horse Guards under my command.

At the outbreak of war the British Army had not paid any serious consideration to the use of pigeons, evidently relying on the field telegraph signals and wireless. The enemy, however, much more adequately prepared for war than the allied forces, had evidently given this subject close consideration as, during the earliest days of the war, both they and the French brought into use a well-organised pigeon service with mobile lofts fully equipped with pigeons.

24

A loft of reserves.

In the defence of Verdun pigeons proved their great value, and were eventually the only means of communication for this front when all other means had failed, and some of the messages sent were of a thrilling nature during February and April, 1916. Following are translations of the actual messages carried from Verdun by pigeons:—

28th February. 14.40. 2 pigeons.

Colonel 166 at (place) Verdun.

"A strong enemy attack has outflanked Champlon and is now directed on the Tresnes Montgirmont Eparges. (Telephonic) cut by a strong bombardment. We are resisting. 334."

29th February. 8.40.

"During the day yesterday and night the bombardment of the position continues. No infantry attack in 1 sector. A deserter gave himself up last night at Bois Carré; according to him the Germans have withdrawn troops to take them to the right bank."

6th March. 17.45.

"Enemy attack continues at Bethincourt at 19.45. Barrage obtained lately has not been able to impede progress.

"About a battalion has been able to concentrate in the woods between Bethincourt and Rafficourt. Artillery has fired on these woods. All communications broken with 1 Brigade.

"(Corbeaux Woods) Bethincourt always held by a battalion of the 220 N. All dispositions taken for holding on Morthomme.

"Very violent bombardment of our lines. Send relief to Souville urgently."

April 16. 6.25 a.m.

"The German counter-attack has been repulsed by the Companies occupying the Hautville Trench and he has entrenched a little in front of his old front. Artillery barrage is necessary on A.U.C. 9x. The 1st Battalion of the 36th is in position a little N. of the Driant Trench. Serious losses, at least 50 per cent. of the effectives. Reinforcements urgent.''

These and other despatches were carried through shell fire and barrage whilst the defence of Verdun held out. It is said the defence of Verdun won the war; if so, pigeons, by their courage, helped to win it.

Major Alec Waley, who was appointed O.C. Carrier-Pigeon Service on the French front, gave some interesting details recently, in an article in the ''Morning Post,'' of the use of pigeons in the battle of the Somme and the important messages carried by them in this great battle. Following extracts are from that article:—

''It was on September 25th that the Guards Division were to attack Les Bœufs and Goudecourt. The pigeon lofts which served this Division were two mobile lofts sited at Minden Post, a few hundred yards behind Carnoy, and thus about ten miles as the pigeon flies from Les Bœufs.

''From early in the morning the pigeon despatch riders had been carrying the birds up in large stock baskets to the different Battalion Headquarters and to the Guards Advanced Division R.C. at Bernafay Wood.

RECORDING THE ADVANCE.

''It was a typical September day, and good for flying, but the artillery preparation was deafening, and tested the birds to the limit. Messages began to come in from 2 p.m., and the regularity with which the birds homed and the advance could be followed was quite remarkable.

Despatch rider with basket of birds.

Birds packed to save jolting, for cavalry use.

Releasing pigeon from aeroplane.

"The messages given below are worth studying. Visualise the conditions under which they were sent, and then picture the two lofts with a few officers and men awaiting the birds. One sees them arriving from afar, over the howitzer batteries before Carnoy; a few circling flights around the lofts, always lower and lower, then with a flutter on to the loft, and then into the trapping box.

"The message-carrier is at once taken off the bird's leg, its little flimsy message form extracted, and the context 'phoned through instantly to Corps and Division H.Q.'s. And then there is a feed for the bird.

In every case R.D. stands for the hour at which the Division received the message, and some were through in remarkable time.

TEXT OF MESSAGES.

"From: Give to Gain. 25/9/16.

"Messages now received from all Companies in Brown Line. Just about to advance to Blue at proper hour. Artillery fire a bit short. Shovels wanted. Have seen Colonel Campbell, and shall proceed myself to village. Resistance feeble.

"Place: Green Line. Time: 2.45 p.m.

"Sender's Signature: R. McCalmont, Lt.-Colonel. R.D.: 3.20 p.m.

"From: Gallant to Gain. 25/9/16.

"Have only one officer left. Could Newton and Transport Officer be sent up to-night Am now advancing through the village of Les Bœufs, supported by 2nd Battalion Coldstreams.

"Sender's Signature: C.M. Time: 2.45 p.m. R.D.: 3.10 p.m.

"From: D. 85 to Z. 8. 25/9/16.

"Message from Welsh Guards reports enemy are turning their left flank, which is not in touch with the 21st Division. A Battalion urgently wanted to fill the gap.

"Place 3. Time: 3.37 p.m.

"Sender's Signature: R. S. Lambert, Capt. R.D.: 3.59 p.m.

"From O.C., L.F. Coy. 2nd Bn. Scots Guards to Great.

"The 2nd Battn. Scots Guards have reached and consolidated their objective. 1st Brigade, on our right, have pushed through Les Bœufs, and are digging themselves in about 50 yards E. side of village. The 21st Division appears to be held up on the left flank of the 4th Grenadiers, who are on the left of this Battalion, and are very badly in the air. For this reason, the left half Battalion First Grenadiers was unable to push on to the 3rd objective, and have now dug themselves in 100 yards behind the 2nd objective. Am trying to establish defensive flank on left 4th Grenadiers. All the Officers of the 4th Grenadiers appear to be casualties.

"Place: N. 33, d.7.3. Time: 3.50 p.m.

"Sender's Signature: V. A. Cochrane Baillie, Lieut. R.D.: 4.25 p.m.

"From: D. 85 to Z. 8. 25/9/16.

"Message received from front line D. 87, 3.15 p.m., reports D. 83 on 3rd objective. D. 87, D. 85 on sunken road, N. 34 A. and D. Troops appear to be echeloned towards the left. Message from left Company, D. 85, 2.15 p.m., reported being at N. 33. D. 22 with their left not in touch with the 21st Division, who are held up on the first German Line. A bombing fight is now in progress on left of D. 89, about N. 32, D.7.4. Situation at that point dangerous.

"Sender's Signature: R. S. Lambert, Capt. Time: 5.15 p.m.

"On this day, on the Somme front alone, over 400 operation mesages came back from tanks and the attacking forces.

"Not a bad record for the pigeons, and a good mark to the stout lads who had to take them up with them over barbed wire, trenches, and shell craters, and so on into the Unknown."

In the Battle of the Somme the French alone used 5,000 pigeons, and only 2 per cent. of the birds released with messages failed to return, notwithstanding shell fire and adverse weather conditions on many occasions. But the loss of 2 per cent. of the pigeons did not mean the failure to deliver any important messages carried, as these were always sent in duplicate on important occasions.

From the tanks pigeons proved of great service to communicate with the base; in fact, were often the only means of communication. Sometimes when liberated from tanks the birds seemed stupified, no doubt due to fumes of the oil, and I strongly recommend the use of small closed baskets for use in the tanks, similar to our show baskets.

We had a loft of instruction for the Tank Corps at Wool, and every officer and man who was to serve in the Tank Corps had to thoroughly master the handling of pigeons.

At the conclusion of the war there were 22,000 pigeons, 150 mobile lofts and, at least, 400 C.P.S. pigeoneers in the C.P.S.

Good reports came from G.H.Q., Salonika, where Sergeant F. Shaw was sent out to establish the service.

The Egyptian service was established by Sergeant H. C. Knott.

In fact, there was not a single unit of the C.P.S. Army Pigeon Service that proved a failure.

After the war a special pamphlet was prepared giving the ring numbers and details of birds that earned special merit. Copies were sent to all owners. The lofts in which the birds were bred were quite unknown to O.C. Pigeons, France. The King's loft had a number of the birds mentioned in despatches. General Shaw handed me for inclusion in my note book the following acknowledgement of the circular:—

> " York Cottage,
>> " Sandringham,
>>> " Norfolk.
> " 28th January, 1918.

" Dear General,

" I have submitted to the King the circular enclosed in your letter of January 26th to Wigram, about the pigeons.

" His Majesty desires me to thank you for sending this, which has interested him very much, and the King is glad to know that some of his birds have been ' mentioned in despatches.'

> " Believe me,
>> " Yours sincerely,
>>> " CROMER.

" Major-General Sir F. C. Shaw, K.C.B."

Shipping the messengers on to a trawler   Naval Service.

Taking birds from gas protector used by Germans

Pigeon with metal message-holder shown on leg.

CHAPTER V

THIS branch of the Carrier-Pigeon Service was only established as a separate entity in 1918, and was organised by Major W. H. Osman, assisted by Capt. E. Burden. Part of the then existing Naval pigeon service was taken over and some part of the Army Carrier-Pigeon Service. There were lofts at all important aerodromes at the conclusion of the war, and pilots learned to feel a confidence in the companionship of a pigeon in its basket in the aerodrome.

In April, 1919, the following letter was issued by command of the Air Council, to be forwarded to all those breeders who had presented birds free of cost for this service.

> "Air Ministry,
>   " Strand,
>   " London, W.C.2.
> "April, 1919.

"HOMING PIGEONS—MERITORIOUS SERVICE " IN ROYAL AIR FORCE.

" Sir,

" I am commanded by the Air Council to forward for your information a list of the ring numbers of pigeons which have rendered meritorious service to the Royal Air Force, with brief details of such performances.

" The Council desire to thank you and all other breeders of homing pigeons who have so generously and patriotically contributed birds to the Pigeon Service, for the valuable assistance which you have rendered thereby to His Majesty's Forces.

" In a large number of cases lives and machines have been saved, and much valuable information has been brought in through the agency of these birds. The list only includes birds which have performed conspicuously good service, but many other pigeons have also done consistently good work.

" I am, Sir,

" Your obedient Servant,

" W. A. ROBINSON."

The following is a copy of the list of meritorious services mentioned in this letter, and as this list gives details of some brilliant performances and lives saved, it will, I think, be sufficient to show the good work of the Air Force Pigeon Service after its establishment as a separate entity. I am unable to embody the work performed by pigeons from this branch of the service prior to 1918, but this I know, that a loft established at Harwich under my command for the use of the Army, and airmen from waterplanes, was the sole means of saving the life of more than one skilled pilot.

In connection with the Harwich loft, which contained about 150 birds constantly in training and at work, it is interesting to note that orders were received to remove Headquarters from Harwich to Felixstowe, about 15 miles to the north of Harwich. I chose the tennis court in front of the Felix Hotel for the new site and men's quarters. In less than ten days after the complete removal of birds and loft all the birds homed from 60 or 70 miles at sea regularly and came straight to Felixstowe without crossing Harwich, and I believe I am right in saying that it was very shortly after this removal one of the Air Force officers was saved by a pigeon message when in desperate straits.

A Life-Saver.—The bird in this photograph carried a message that saved the lives of six airmen.

PARTICULARS OF MERITORIOUS SERVICES IN ROYAL AIR FORCE.

Ring Nos.	Colour.	Sex.	Remarks.
3 N.U.R.P. 17 O.	Cheq.	Cock	Has done consistently good work.
4 N.U.R.P. 17 O.	Blue Cheq.	Cock	Has done consistently good work.
6 N.U.R.P. 17 O.	Mealy Pied	Cock	Arrived home through thick mist with message, "Landed through engine trouble, being towed by T.B.D. 92."
13 N.U.H.P. 17 Z.	Cheq., White Flights	Hen	Has done consistently good work.
42 N.U.H.P. 16 F.D.	White Grizzle	Cock	Brought message from Seaplane in distress 65 miles at sea.
45 N.U. 17 G.P.S.	Dark Cheq.	Cock	Has done large amount of long distance work, through heavy mists at sea. Always reliable.
56 N.U. 17 G.P.S.	Blue Cheq.	Cock	Has done consistently good work.
60 N.U. 17 G.P.S.	Dark Cheq.	Cock	Seaplane down on water with engine trouble. First news came from pigeon message, and assistance was sent.
77 N.U. 17 G.P.S.	Blue Cheq.	Cock	Has done consistently good work.
94 R.P. 17 S.U.B.	Blue Cheq.	Cock	Completed 100 Active Service Patrols.
104 N.U. 17 G.P.S.	Blue Cheq.	Cock	Liberated from Seaplane in difficulties, the message carried being the means of saving the lives of the Pilot and Observer. This bird has repeatedly done good work.
119 N.U.H.P. 17 Y.	Cheq. Pied	Cock	This bird h s flown very consistently throughout, and has brought in messages on several occasions under various weather conditions.
186 N.U. 17 G.P.S.	Blue	Hen	Brought message that machine was forced to land, had crashed and was sinking.

Ring Nos.	Colour	Sex	Remarks.
232 N.U.R.P. 14 O.	Blue Cheq.	Cock	Seaplane down on water 45 miles from base. This pigeon brought the message giving the position, and assistance was sent.
234 N.U. 17 G.P.S.	—		Has returned with messages.
243 N.U. 16 W.C.F.	Blue Cheq.	Cock	Completed 130 Active Service Patrols.
273 N.U.R.P. 17 F.	Pied Cheq.	Cock	Has brought in messages on several occasions in adverse circumstances.
296 N.U.H.P. 16 S.F.C.	Black	Cock	Brought message saying machine on water, sinking. When found, crew had been in the water for over two hours, sitting on the upturned floats.
376 S.N.L. 14	Dark Blue	Hen	The lives of the Pilot and Observer of a Seaplane were saved as a result of a message brought in by this bird, through very adverse weather conditions, but despite the dense fog prevailing this bird arrived home. A Torpedo Boat, after much trouble owing to the fog, succeeded in picking up the Pilot and Observer. They had been on the water 12 hours.
408 N.U. 11 C.H.	Blue Cheq.	Cock	Liberated in heavy thunderstorm 22 miles N.E. of Loft, at 6.44 a.m. Homed at 7.9 a.m. reporting result of fight with enemy machines.
419 S.U. 16 A.	Blue Pied	Hen	Has returned with messages.
468 N.U.R.P. 17 F.	Blue Cheq.	Cock	Has done consistently good work.
470 N.U.R.P. 17 F.	Cheq.	Hen	Has done consistently good work.
482 N.U.R.P. 17 F.	Blue Cheq.	Cock	This bird has flown very consistently throughout, and has brought in messages on several occasions in various weather conditions.
483 N.U.R.P. 17 F.	Blue Cheq.	Cock	Liberated 160 miles from land at 6.30 p.m. *in darkness and fog*, and reached the station in good time.
485 N.U.R.P. 17 F.	Blue Cheq.	Cock	The last bird to be liberated from a total wreck 190 miles at sea on a dark, stormy December night, with a 30-knot wind dead against him. He arrived at the Loft with message early next morning.

Ring Nos.	Colour	Sex	Remarks
492 H.P. 16 M.	Red Cheq.	Cock	Has completed 172 Active Service Patrols.
602 R.P. 17 S.U.G.F.	Dark Blue Cheq.	Hen	Liberated from Seaplane forced to land, giving position of wreck and requesting immediate help. This message was the first intimation received.
606 S.U.R.P. 17 G.F.	Red Cheq.	Cock	Seaplane crashed about 10 miles from base, and this bird, although almost drowned, returned with message in time for assistance to be sent. All the crew were saved. Brought messages for help during November, 1917, under bad weather conditions. In February, 1918, returned from 50 miles in 1¼ hours with message from large Seaplane in distress. Crew were saved.
607 N.U.R.P. 17 F.	Pied	Hen	The message carried by this bird was that a Seaplane was down with engine trouble 40 miles from Base. This was the means of same being safely brought back in tow.
639 R.P. 14 O.F.	Blue Cheq.	Cock	(a) Liberated in July at 11.0 a.m., after 18 days in the basket, and homed at 11.48. (b) Liberated in moonlight, 1.0 a.m. September, 5 miles N.W. of Loft. Homed at 1.30 a.m.
672 N.U.R.P. 17 L.	Red Cheq.	Hen	Has done consistently good work.
702 N.U.R.P. 17 E.J.	Red Pied	Cock	Duplicate of message carried by 6 N.U.R.P. 17 O.
735 N.U.R.P. 17 U.N.	Cheq.	Hen	Has done consistently good work.
762 N.U.R.P. 17 E.J.	Blue Cheq.	Hen	Has returned with messages.
852 N.U.R.P. 16 H.	Red Cheq.	Cock	Liberated from Seaplane bringing this valuable information: "We have come down with engine trouble. Top of radiator come adrift. Engine practically seized up."
888 H.P. 14 A.	Dark Blue Cheq.	Cock	Meritorious long service is shown by this pigeon, which has been flying continuously for 18 months in all weathers, and has carried many messages of urgency and importance.

Ring Nos.	Colour.	Sex.	Remarks.
897 N.U.R.P. 17 E.J. ..	Blue Cheq.	Hen ..	Has done consistently good work.
922 R.P. 17 E.J.	Blue Cheq.	Cock ..	Liberated from Seaplane down on sea 60 miles from station.
951 N.U.R.P. 17 F. ..	Red Cheq.	Cock ..	Liberated from Seaplane 35 miles from Base with this message: "Down in Black Deep Channel in rough sea. Pressure did not hold. T.B.D. coming up."
952 N.U.R.P. 17 F. ..	Blue Cheq.	Cock ..	Was liberated approximately 70 miles from Loft on a bad day and returned to Loft in exceptionally fast time. This bird has a very good record.
958 N.U. 1 L.S.V. ..	Grizzle ..	Cock ..	Has completed 146 Active Service Patrols.
984 R.P. S. 13 F. ..	Blue	Hen ..	Has done consistently good work.
998 N.U.R.P. 16 M.C. ..	Cheq.	Hen ..	Has done consistently good work.
1087 N.U.R.P. 17 P. ..	Dark Cheq.	Hen ..	Liberated with message asking for assistance 50 miles out at sea, and returned in 1½ hours against strong wind.
1132 N.U.R.P. 17 E.J. ..	Blue Cheq.	Cock ..	A Seaplane was forced to land through engine trouble. Pigeon message resulted in assistance being sent, and machine being brought back in tow.
1133 R.P. 16 X.	—	—	Liberated at 1 a.m. and homed with message from Seaplane down at sea.
1176 N.U. 18 G.P.S. ..	—	—	Returned with message from Airship, arriving at Loft badly wounded in back.
1178 N.U. 18 G.P.S. ..	—	—	Has returned with messages.
1241 N.U. 18 G.P.S. ..	Dark Cheq.	Hen ..	Brought back message that machine was forced to land in the sea. As the result a destroyer was directed to search for the Pilot, and he was picked up, his machine having sunk 15 minutes after landing.
1259 N.U.R.P. 17 F. ..	Blue Pied	Cock ..	This bird has flown very consistently throughout, and has brought in messages on several occasions in various weather conditions.

86

A Convoy of Reinforcements for France outside Doughty Street before the start.

Left to right (Back): G. Ainsworth, A. Etchells, J. H. Abram, R. C. Rich, W. Claridge, G. Howard, D. Soinerville, S. Sams.
Middle: S. J. Passey, T. Farrow, E. W. Steele, R. Rimmer, W. Jordan.
Front: J. Master, W. Rimmer, G. W. Wright, W. Wilson.

Ring Nos.	Colour		Remarks
1261 N.U.R.P. 17 F.	Blue Cheq. Pied	Cock	Liberated in thick fog and arrived home in quick time. On three other occasions has done long flights in very good time under adverse circumstances.
1274 N.U.R.P. 17 F.	Blue Pied	Cock	Has returned with messages.
1305 N.U. 16 L.C.	Blue	Cock	Brought in this valuable information: "Down, both planes broken."
1331 N.U.H.P. 16 Z.	Cheq.	Hen	Has done consistently good work.
1332 N.U.R.P. 17 K.	Red Cheq.	Cock	Worked consistently on several occasions.
1346 R.P. 14 N.	—	—	Brought message reporting forced landing.
1409 N.U.R.P. 16 S.	Blue Cheq., White Flights	Cock	Brought back following message: "Down in rough sea." Motor launch was despatched and pilot and observer were landed at 9.30 p.m.
1432 N.U.R.P. 17 E.J.	Black Cheq.	Cock	Liberated 35 miles from base. Homed in one hour carrying following message: "Torpedo boat coming alongside. Very heavy sea running. Machine not damaged. Floats not leaking."
1539 N.U.R.P. 17 F.	Blue Cheq.	Hen	Has returned with messages.
1562 N.U.R.P. 17 F.	Cheq.	Hen	Has done consistently good work.
1568 R.P. 17 E.J.	Blue	Hen	Carried many messages through fogs and heavy mists, always in excellent time.
1652 N.U.R.P. 17 E.J.	Blue Cheq.	Cock	This bird has flown very consistently throughout, and has brought in messages on several occasions in various weather conditions.
1722 N.U.R.P. 16 F.S.	Blue Cheq.	Hen	Has returned with messages.
1878 N.U.R.P. 17 F.	Blue Pied	Cock	This bird has flown very consistently throughout, and has brought in messages on several occasions under various weather conditions.
1911 N.U.R.P. 17 F.	Red	Cock	Brought duplicate of message carried by 7177 N.U.R.P. 17 F.
2121 N.U.H.P. 17 Y.	Cheq.	Cock	Has done consistently good work.

Ring Nos.	Colour.	Sex.	Remarks.
2171 N.U.R.P. 17 F.	Blue Cheq.	—	Brought back message: "Two Seaplanes down on water, unable to fly." A Motor Launch was sent to their assistance.
2193 R.P. 16 F.S. ..	—	—	Brought message reporting saving of Pilot down at sea.
2278 R.P. 17 E.J. ..	Blue Cheq.	Hen	Liberated from Short Seaplane with message, "Landed owing to engine trouble." Returned with crop cut open.
2450 N.U.R.P. 11 O.	Blue	Cook	Has done consistently good work.
2463 N.U.R.P. 15 M.	Blue Cheq.	Hen	Duplicate of message carried by 852 N.U.R.P. 16 H.
2533 N.U.R.P. 17 E.J.	Blue	Cock	Has returned with messages.
2657 N.U.R.P. 17 F.	Mealy	Cock	This bird has flown very consistently throughout, and has brought in messages on several occasions in various weather conditions.
2658 N.U.R.P. 17 L.P.	Cheq.	Hen	Has done consistently good work.
2659 N.U.R.P. 17 L.P.	Cheq.	Hen	Has done consistently good work.
2667 N.U.R.P. 16 F.S.	Grizzle	Cook	Has flown exceptionally well on many occasions, and proved itself a most consistent bird.
2746 N.U.R.P. 16 F.S.	—	—	Liberated at sea with message 3.30 a.m., returned to Loft at 3.50 a.m.
2764 N.U.R.P. 17 F.	Pied	Cook	Has done consistently good work.
2930 R.P. 17 M.C...	Blue	Cook	Has done large amount of long distance work, through heavy mists at sea. Speedy and reliable.
2936 N.U.R.P. 17 F.	Blue Cheq. Pied	Cook	Has done large amount of long distance work, through heavy mists at sea. Speedy and reliable.
3018 N.U.R.P. 17 F.	Blue Cheq.	Cock	Has done consistently good work.
3037 : :	Mealy ..	Hen	Liberated with message from Seaplane down with engine trouble 30 miles from base. Pilot and Observer stated that the information conveyed by the pigeon was the means of their being rescued.

Ring Nos.	Colour.	Sex.	Remarks.
3046 N.U.R.P. 16 F.S.	Blue Pied	Hen	Liberated with message from Seaplane: "Engine failed suddenly."
3093 R.P. 17 F.	Blue Cheq.	Cock	Liberated from Aeroplane with message: "Have been forced to land through engine trouble. Machine wrecked."
3100 N.U.R.P. 16 F.S.	Black	Hen	Duplicate of message carried by 1409 N.U.R.P. 16 S.
3145 N.U. 16 M.C.	Blue	Hen	Brought message from Seaplane: "Down, engine trouble."
3165 N.U.R.P. 17 E.J.	Black Cheq.	Cock	Brought this message through thick mist: "Landed, engine trouble. Taxiing home. Send Motor Launch—getting worse."
3168 N.U.R.P. 17 F.	Dark Blue Cheq.	Cock	Brought in messages under various weather conditions.
3253 N.U.R.P. 17 E.J.	Red Cheq.	Hen	Has done consistently good work.
3460 N.U.R.P. 17 E.J.	Blue Cheq.	Hen	Has returned with messages.
3480 N.U.R.P. 17 E.J.	Cheq.	Hen	Has done consistently good work.
3515 R.P. 17 F.	Blue Cheq., White Flights	Cock	Liberated from Seaplane forced to land. Machine and Pilot towed back.
3534 N.U.R.P. 17 F.	Red Cheq.	Cock	Seaplane failed to return. The first news came from the message carried by this pigeon from 100 miles at sea, with the result that the crew of six were saved after being on the water three days.
3680 N.U.R.P. 16 F.S.	Black	Hen	Has done good and consistent work.
3698 N.U.R.P. 17 F.	Blue	Cock	Known as "Pilot's Luck," brought back valuable information, stating "Seaplane badly damaged," and giving her position. Was also liberated 200 miles from base and delivered its message in five hours. Message ran: "Down on water with engine trouble, being attacked by three enemy machines." This was the first intimation of danger received.

Ring Nos.	Colour.	Sex.	Remarks.
3738 N.U.R.P. 17 F.	Blue Cheq.	Cock	Has done consistently good work.
3803 N.U.R.P. 17 E.J.	Cheq.	Hen	Has done consistently good work.
3847	Dark Cheq.	Hen	Duplicate of message carried by 3037.
4173 N.U.R.P. 18 F.	Red Cheq.	Hen	Has done consistently good work.
4230 R.P. 10	Cheq. Pied.	—	Duplicate of message carried by 376 S.N.L. 14.
4315 R.P. 16 F.	Red Cheq.	Cock	Has completed 168 Active Service Patrols.
4684 N.U.R.P. 17 F.	Red Cheq.	Cock	Has returned with messages.
5148 N.U.R.P. 17 F.	Blue Cheq.	Cock	This bird has flown very consistently throughout, and has brought in messages on several occasions under various weather conditions.
5150 N.U.R.P. 17 F.	Cheq.	Hen	Has done consistently good work.
5570 N.U.R.P. 17 F.	Red Cheq.	Cock	Returned with message from Seaplane 40 miles away in one hour.
5583 N.U.R.P. 17 F.	Blue Cheq.	Hen	Returned with message that Seaplane was "Down, totally disabled, 45 miles from base." As a result the crew and machine were brought back safely in tow.
5804 N.U.R.P. 17 F.	Blue	Cock	Has done consistently good work.
5945 N.U.R.P. 16 X.	Blue Cheq.	Hen	Liberated from an Airship which was forced to descend at sea. This was the first intimation of the ship being in distress.
6604 N.U.R.P. 16 H.	Red Cheq.	Hen	Brought this message from Seaplane: "In tow of T.B.D. 2. Send Motor Launch to meet us. Position now D. 3 buoy."
6663 R.P. 17 F.	Red Cheq.	Cock	Brought duplicate of message carried by 17525 R.P. 17 F.
6665 R.P. 17 F.	Blue Cheq.	Cock	Duplicate of message carried by 3515 R.P. 17 F.
6714 N.U.R.P. 17 F.	Blue Cheq.	Cock	Liberated in thick fog over 100 miles from Loft, and arrived home in quick time. Most consistent bird.
6752 N.U.R.P. 17 F.	Blue Cheq.	Cock	Has done consistently good work.

Despatch riders leaving Horse Guards' lofts with pigeons.

A few lofts, somewhere in France, waiting to be stocked.

Ring Nos.	Colour	Sex	Remarks.
6811 N.U.R.P. 17 F.	Blue	Cock ..	This bird has flown very consistently throughout, and has brought messages on several occasions under various weather conditions.
7177 N.U.R.P. 17 F.	Black	Cock ..	Flew 53 miles in 50 minutes with message: ' own All O.K. Please send tow.''
7359 N.U.R.P. 17 F.	Blue Cheq. ..	Cock ..	Has done consistently good work.
7360 N.U.R.P. 17 F.	Blue Cheq. ..	Cock ..	Has done consist..ly good work.
7374 N.U.R.P. 17 F.	Blue Cheq. ..	Cock ..	Has done consistently good work.
7375 N.U.R.P. 17 F.	Cheq.	Hen ..	Has done consistently good work.
7517 N.U.R.P. 17 F.	Blue Cheq. ..	Cock ..	This bird has flown very consistently, and has brought messages on several occasions under various weather conditions.
7661 N.U.R.P. 16 S.	Mealy	Cock ..	Brought last message from Short machine, shot down off Ostend. Had previously brought several messages in good time.
7818 R.P. 17 F. ..	Blue Pied ..	Cock ..	Carried many messages through fogs and heavy mists, always in excellent time.
7822 N.U.R.P. 17 F.	Blue Cheq. ..	Cock ..	Brought duplicate of message carried by 5583 N.U.R.P. 17 F.
7874 N.U.R.P. 17 F.	Red Cheq. ..	Cock ..	Has done consistently good work.
8114 R.P. 17 F. ..	Black	Cock ..	Carried many messages through fog and heavy mist, always in excellent time.
8129 H.P. 13 C. ..	Dark Blue ..	Hen ..	Meritorious long service is shown by this pigeon, which has been flying continuously for 18 months in all weathers, and has carried many messages of urgency and importance.
8197 H.P. 14 C. ..	Dark Blue Cheq.	Hen ..	Meritorious long service is shown by this pigeon, which has been flying continuously for 18 months in all weathers, and has carried many messages of urgency and importance.
8521 N.U.R.P. 17 F.	Blue Cheq. ..	Cock ..	Has done consistently good work.

Ring Nos.	Colour.	Sex.	Remarks.
8591 N.U.R.P. 18 F.	Red Cheq.	Hen	Machine forced to land. Pigeon flew through heavy thunderstorm in high wind, conveying first intimation of forced landing.
8614 N.U.R.P. 17 F.	Cheq.	Hen	Has done consistently good work.
8618 N.U.R.P. 17 F.	Red Cheq.	Cock	Has done consistently good work.
8619 N.U.R.P. 17 F.	Blue	Cock	Has done consistently good work.
8665 N.U.R.P. 17 F.	Dark Cheq.	Hen	Has brought several messages in time for nests to be sent to Seaplanes.
9339 N.U.R.P. 17 F.	Blue Cheq.	Cock	Has done consistently good work.
9372 N.U.R.P. 17 F.	Blue Cheq.	Cock	Has done consistently good work.
9389 N.U.R.P. 17 F.	Cheq.	Hen	Has done consistently good work.
9523 N.U.R.P. 17 F.	Cheq.	Hen	Has done consistently good work.
9645 N.U.R.P. 17 F.	Blue Cheq.	Hen	Has returned with messages.
9848 N.U.R.P. 16 H.	Blue Cheq.	Hen	Has done consistently good work.
9910 N.U.R.P. 17 F.	Blue	Hen	Has done consistently good work.
9938 R.P. 17 F.	Blue Pied	Hen	Liberated from Short Seaplane on patrol, with important information.
9995 N.U.R.P. 16 B.	Mealy	Cock	Has returned with messages.
10695 N.U.R.P. 17 F.	Cheq.	Cock	Has returned with messages.
10982 N.U.R.P. 17 F.	Blue Cheq.	Cock	Has done consistently good work.
10989 N.U.R.P. 17 F.	Cheq.	Hen	Has done consistently good work.
11015 N.U.R.P. 17 F.	Blue Cheq.	Cock	Has returned with messages.
11149 N.U.R.P. 17 F.	Red Cheq.	Cock	Has returned with messages.
11202 N.U.R.P. 17 F.	—	Hen	Duplicate of message brought by 607 N.U.R.P. 17 F.
11203 N.U.R.P. 17 F.	Pied	Hen	Has done consistently good work.
11204 N.U.R.P. 17 F.	Pied	Hen	Has done consistently good work.
12529 N.U.R.P. 17 F.	Cheq.	Cock	Has returned with messages.
12736 N.U.R.P. 17 F.	Blue Cheq.	Hen	Has returned with messages.
12877 R.P. 17 F.	Blue Cheq.	Cock	Has done much continuous work, speedy and reliable.
12988 N.U.R.P. 17 F.	Blue Cheq. Pied	Hen	Brought messages from Seaplane 100 miles from Loft. Has done consistently good work.
13096 N.U.R.P. 17 F.	Blue Cheq.	Cock	Has consistently done good work.

42

A stationary loft, showing temporary outside flight attached when removed to new post.

A mobile loft with birds on top.

Ring Nos.	Colour	Sex	Remarks.
13138 N.U.R.P. 17 F.	Blue Cheq.	Cook	Has consistently done good work.
13138 N.U.R.P. 17 F.	Cheq.	Hen	Has consistently done good work.
13517 N.U.R.P. 17 F.	Cheq.	Hen	Has consistently done good work.
13520 R.P. 17 F.	Grizzle	Hen	Carried many messages through fogs and heavy mists, always in excellent time.
13526 N.U.R.P. 17 F.	Blue Cheq.	Hen	Has returned with messages.
14085 R.P. 17 F.	Blue	Cook	Duplicate of message carried by 3093 R.P. 17 F.
14156 R.P. 17 F.	Black, White Flights	Cook	Carried many messages through fogs and heavy mists, always in excellent time.
14176 N.U.R.P. 17 F.	Cheq.	Hen	Has done consistently good work.
14177 N.U.R.P. 17 F.	Cheq.	Hen	Has done consistently good work.
14181 N.U.R.P. 17 F.	Cheq.	Hen	Has done consistently good work.
14206 N.U.R.P. 17 F.	Blue Cheq.	Cook	Has done consistently good work.
14299 N.U.R.P. 17 F.	Cheq.	Hen	Has done consistently good work.
14520 N.U.R.P. 18 F.	Blue Cheq.	Cook	Has done consistently good work.
15050 N.U.R.P. 17 F.	Blue	Cook	Has done good work on a number of occasions—all under trying circumstances.
15134 N.U.R.P. 17 F.	Dark Cheq.	Cook	Has been liberated on several occasions with important messages, and in spite of very bad weather conditions has returned in good time.
15540 R.P. 17 F.	Red	Cook	Liberated from Seaplane with important information.
15610 R.P. 17 F.	Blue Pied	Hen	Liberated from Short Seaplane with message: "Landed owing to engine trouble."
15744 N.U.R.P. 18 F.	Blue Cheq.	Cook	Following message brought in by this pigeon: "Down, send assistance at once." This was the first intimation received, and was the means of saving the crew and the machine. On several other occasions this pigeon has brought back valuable information.
16119 N.U.R.P. 17 F.	Blue	Hen	This bird has flown very consistently throughout, and has brought in messages on several occasions under various weather conditions.

Ring Nos.	Colour.	Sex.	Remarks.
16331 N.U.R.P. 17 F.	Mealy ..	Cock	Liberated with duplicate of message carried by 3534 N.U.R.P. 17 F. Was picked up dead a few miles from the Loft, having died from exhaustion.
16407 N.U.R.P. 17 F.	—	—	Has returned with messages.
16450 N.U.R.P. 17 F.	Cheq. ..	Cock	Has done consistently good work; speedy and reliable.
16564 R.P. 17 F. ..	Blue Cheq.	Cock	Helpless on the water, the Pilot and Observer sent these pigeons with the following message: "We can hear firing, but cannot see land or ships.
17291 N.U.R.P. 17 F.	Dark Blue ..	Cock	Can you send round coast about 21 miles or so out. We really have no knowledge of our position
17293 N.U.R.P. 17 F.	Dark Blue Cheq.	Cock	at all. Very urgent. Both feeling very, very faint. Perhaps we are off the southern coast. Compass no use."
17404 N.U.R.P. 17 F.	Cheq. ..	Hen	Has done consistently good work.
17525 R.P. 17 F. ..	Mealy ..	Hen	Liberated with message from Seaplane forced to land. Machine and Pilot towed back.
17677 N.U.R.P. 18 F.	Red Cheq.	Hen	Duplicate of message carried by 8591 N.U.R.P. 18 F.
17837 N.U.R.P. 17 F.	Cheq. ..	Hen	Has done consistently good work.
17984 N.U.R.P. 17 F.	Blue Cheq.	Cock	Has done consistently good work.
17989 N.U.R.P. 17 F.	Blue Cheq.	Cock	This bird has flown very consistently throughout, and has brought in messages on several occasions through various weather conditions.
18112 N.U.R.P.F.	Blue ..	Hen	Duplicate of message carried by 1241 N.U. 18 G.P.S.
18793 N.U.R.P. 17 F.	Blue (Frill)	Hen	Liberated 1¼ hours before daybreak at sea with message. Homed immediately after daybreak.
18835 N.U.R.P. 18 F.	Blue Cheq.	Cock	Has done consistently good work.
20279 R.P. 17 F. ..	Black ..	—	Duplicate of message carried by 2171 N.U.R.P. 17 F.
21166 N.U.R.P. 18 F.	Blue Cheq.	Hen	Has done consistently good work.

Ring Nos.	Colour.	Sex.	Remarks.
21184 N.U.R.P. 18 F.	Blue Cheq.	Cock	Brought message that machine was forced to land well out of sight of land. Owing to thick fog, the Pilot had lost his bearings.
21376 N.U.R.P. 17 F.	Blue Cheq.	Hen	Liberated with message requesting help, having flown 22 miles in 22 minutes. This message was the first intimation of the crew being in difficulties.
21438	Red Cheq.	Cock	Has done consistently good work.
21454	—	—	Liberated with message that Seaplane was down with engine trouble. First intimation received by station.
22038 N.U.R.P. 17 F.	—	Hen	Duplicate of message carried by 602 R.P. 17 S.U.G.F.
23371 N.U.R.P. 18 F.	Blue Cheq.	—	Seaplane was shot down in flames by five enemy machines, about 30 miles from base. This pigeon brought the message, and three of the crew were saved, after being in the water three-quarters of an hour.
64441 N.U.R.P. 18 F.	Red Cheq.	Hen	Liberated later by Pilot who despatched 186 N.U. 17 G.P.S., with message that he was aboard a trawler, and machine being salved.
243 N.U. 16 W.C.F.	Blue Cheq.	Cock	These birds between them have been on continuous service, and between October, 1916, and November, 1918, have done 801 Active Service Patrols and Bomb Raids into enemy country.
492 H.P. 16 M.	Red Cheq.	Cock	
958 N.U. 15 L.V.	Grizzle	Cock	
4315 R.P. 16 E.	Red Cheq.	Cock	
4502 R.P. 16 B.	Red Cheq.	Cock	
5022 H.P. 14 B.N.	Black Cheq.	Hen	
94 R.P. 17 S.U.A.	Blue Cheq.	Hen	
151 H.P. 17 U.F.	Black	Cock	
152 H.P. 17 U.F.	Black	Cock	
295 R.P. 17 O.	Blue Cheq.	Hen	These birds between them have done 604 Active Service Patrols during 1917 and 1918.
2288 H.P. 17 J.	Blue Cheq. Pied	Cock	
10042 R.P. 17 F.	Blue Cheq.	Cock	
14325 R.P. 17 F.	Mealy	Cock	

45

CHAPTER VI

AFTER being attached to R.E. Signals in the early stages of the organisation of the Carrier-Pigeon Service, I was eventually attached to the Intelligence Corps, and I feel that it was in this work that our pigeons added to their value in the silent and efficient messenger work they performed.

Here is one of the uses to which pigeons were put :—

A small balloon was constructed with a metal band worked by clockwork. To this band was attached a small basket containing a single pigeon with a message holder on its leg, and to each basket was attached a small parachute. The balloons were liberated in favourable conditions of wind and at intervals automatically released from the special ring a single basket with a bird. These were dropped into Belgian and French territory when occupied by the Germans, and in French and Flemish a request was made to the finder to supply intelligence information that was needed, at the same time giving the finder hopefulness and cheer as to the ultimate success of the allies' cause and promising reward for the information supplied.

Much valuable information was obtained in this manner.

Major Alec. Waley, M.C.
O.C. Pigeons, France.

Capt. E. E. Jackson.
O.C. C.P.S., Ireland.

Capt. Gerald Lockett.

Lieut. F. Romer, O.B.E.

So alarmed did the Germans become at its success that they took every possible means to detect those who had the courage to send messages.

The following notice was placarded throughout Belgium in French and Flemish:—

"The enemy is in the habit of dropping from aeroplanes little baskets containing homing pigeons, by means of which they desire to obtain information concerning this side of the line.

"The pigeons are placed in small baskets and marked 'Please open.'

"Any person who finds one of these baskets must, without tampering with it, report to the nearest military authorities. All persons are forbidden to open baskets or any letters attached to them, or to remove them from the place where they are found.

"Inhabitants disobeying these orders are liable to the severest punishment. If they attempt to escape they run the risk of being shot instantly.

"Any town in which one of these pigeons is secreted is liable to a fine of 10,000 to 100,000 francs."

In addition to the issue of this proclamation, the Germans set a trap for those who might find pigeons and be tempted to use them.

They removed the pigeon dropped by us and substituted a bird that would home to their own lofts, so that if anyone was foolish enough to attach his name and address to the message the pigeon would deliver it to them and the person be arrested and shot.

For this reason we warned persons in our instructions never to use any names for identity and always to liberate the birds at night so that they would home to our lofts in the morning.

This method succeeded for a time, but later we had to decide upon other methods. It was then decided that our airmen should carry a brave Belgian willing to descend with a basket of pigeons by parachute dark at night when a favourable position for his descent was reached. Men were found brave enough to undertake this risk for their King and country—naturally Belgians who knew where to hide in safety.

For this service I designed a special basket of the shape of a fisherman's creel that strapped on the back. I carefully wrapped the pigeons in paper and packed them in straw.

The scheme was a success, except that at the outset great difficulty was experienced in getting the man to jump from the plane when the time came.

The basket was on the man's back and the parachute strapped round his armpits.

A special aeroplane was designed in order that when the position was reached the seat upon which the man sat gave way automatically when the pilot let go a lever and the man was let out to gracefully parachute to earth.

In almost all cases this scheme proved most successful, but on one occasion the aeroplane crashed, killing one of the men. The other tossed all the pigeons, and news was received of the disaster.

It was not merely necessary to obtain messages that could be sent by flimsies, but much larger plans or even passports were needed. The carriage of larger objects than the ordinary message presented some difficulty, when I was approached with this object, but I decided that the tail of the bird should be used as the carrier.

I threaded a piece of fine wire through the outside tail feathers on each side, leaving two loose ones to come underneath. One piece of wire was threaded through the strongest tail feathers near the root of the tail and another piece about 2 inches lower down the tail in the same manner.

The package to be sent was wired round with two thin pieces of wire the same distance apart and then attached to the loose wires under the tail. A whole sheet of the "Daily Mail" can easily be sent a reasonable distance in this manner.

Our agents over the enemy lines would flash a signal at night. Relays of pigeons would be dropped. The message or parcel would be at once attached to the pigeon, which would be immediately liberated and home at its loft in the morning.

The Germans boasted of their intelligence service, but our pigeon service was as good as any during the war.

Knowing the extent to which we used pigeons for intelligence work is it surprising that it was deemed necessary that every precaution should be taken to prevent the promiscuous liberation of pigeons in this country during the war.

On one occasion, on boarding a foreign steamer from a neutral country off Newcastle, a dozen racing pigeons were found. But the skipper had them killed promptly on our men discovering them, and said he always carried live pigeons to kill for food. Mr. Basil Thompson's men were a little slow in not getting these pigeons alive, when we might have used them to send the enemy some "useful" news.

The German message holders used for their service were very finely manufactured. We often captured pigeons, but few of their message holders.

When one was obtained, I got Carter, of Birmingham, to imitate them so perfectly that it was impossible to distinguish the original, and a trick was often played on Fritz by sending him a few bogus messages with his own pigeons we captured.

At the outbreak of war the Belgians had no doubt the finest pigeon service in the world, with headquarters in Antwerp, but before the capture of Antwerp, on October 8th, 1914, Commandant Denuit, chief of the Belgian service, had the lofts and birds all destroyed, thus preventing the Germans using a service that had taken years to become efficient.

The Intelligence Pigeon Service designed for home use in case of invasion was a magnificent one. Day after day the birds were kept ready, winter and summer, but thank God this branch of the service was never called upon to prove its value. Had it been, the birds would have given the enemy cause to respect its efficiency.

Much of the good work that pigeons did for the Intelligence Service must of necessity remain untold, but for espionage the pigeon will ever be a grave danger, as well as great value to those who make the best use of them, as was the case in the Great War.

Red Cock, known as "Crisp, V.C." (See page 21).

"Pilot's Luck"—Carried message from airman attacked 200 miles at sea,
and safely delivered message.

CHAPTER VII

It was in August, 1917, that I first met officers from the American Army attached to pigeons. I found them intelligent and keen to take advantage of information derived from our past experience. The first American Pigeon Service consisted of two officers and 12 men selected from prominent American pigeon men. At the end of the Armistice the American Army pigeon service consisted of 9 officers, 324 soldiers, 6,000 pigeons and 50 mobile lofts.

So impressed was the Signal Service of the American Army with the use to which pigeons could be put, that upon the conclusion of the Armistice a service was established and is still maintained at good strength in America.

I am reminded of my cordial association with American officers and men by the following letter:—

       " War Department,

      " Office of the Chief Signal Officer,

         " Washington.

       " September 12th, 1919.

" My dear Colonel Osman,

  " It has been brought to my attention that on several occasions during the war and since the signing of the Armistice you have been of the greatest assistance to the Pigeon Section of the Signal Corps in the furtherance of its interests. Due to your efforts every courtesy and opportunity for instruction were accorded the American pigeoneers who visited the British armies for observation purposes.

" The voluntary gift of six hundred young pigeons from the British fanciers to the American Army was most opportune and significant of the splendid feeling that existed between the two armies. Furthermore, the selection of the three hundred pigeons purchased by you recently for the stocking of United States government lofts must have made great demands on your time and personal influence.

" On behalf of the Signal Corps, I desire to express fullest acknowledgment of the value of your services, and appreciation of the fine spirit of co-operation and goodwill that prompted them.

" Very truly yours,

" GEORGE O. SQUIER,

" Major-General,
" Chief Signal Officer of the Army.

" Lieutenant-Colonel A. H. Osman,

" 19, Doughty Street,

" London, W.C.1,

" England."

The following letter from General Fowler to General Shaw will give some idea of the smooth working of the Service. General Shaw gave me the letter and photos to put amongst my collection.

" General Headquarters,

France.

" 1st April, 1917.

" My dear Shaw,

" The sending of the pigeons from England to France has worked very smoothly and successfully. We have got a very good lot of birds, and there have been hardly any casualties, which shows the great care that must have been taken in England in selecting and consigning them.

" I enclose two photos of the horse-drawn pigeon lofts collected at Boulogne to receive the pigeons. Osman might like to see the photos. I do not want them back.

" As each consignment of pigeons arrived they were put in the lofts and drawn off to their positions on the front, where I hope they will very soon be in work.

"A good many have gone up to the areas where we have advanced, and it was very important to get the early young birds so as to make this possible.

"As to future requirements, the balance still due of the first 5,000 we asked for had better come about the 21st April, by which time we shall know if any lofts have failed and require re-stocking.

"We have asked officially for 1,000 to be available in May and 1,000 in June, and I expect that these will be used to establish lofts in new areas or to make good casualties in old lofts.

" Very many thanks for all the care that has been taken to get good birds.

" Yours,

" JOHN FOWLER."

The Italians had a very large force of carrier pigeons. A service that grew as the war progressed, and the great value of this branch of the signal service was recognised. Before the great retreat of 1917 the Italians had upwards of 30,000 birds in use. Later, this number was increased to 50,000, in addition to which civilian lofts in Italy were requisitioned, and at least 2,000 birds from these lofts were on active service. When the Italian Army was on the Piave in June, 1918, 1,500 Italians were surrounded and in great danger from the Austrian attack. Two pigeons were then liberated at night with a message for help and giving details of the enemy positions. As the result of these two messages, reinforcements were at once sent and the Italian beseiged men rescued, 3,500 Austrians being taken prisoners.

In Ireland an efficient and useful service was organised, Capt. E. E. Jackson being placed in charge. All lorries travelling any distance between different depots carried pigeons and, thanks to this system, when an officer who had been captured escaped he was able to reach a lorry, have pigeons sent to say he was on board, and just when an attempt was made to recapture him, a mobile force of motor-cyclists arrived and put paid to the attackers. Captain Rayner succeeded Captain Jackson in charge of the Irish service until order was restored in that country.

Part of my duty was to inspect all lofts and lecture to Cadet and other Signal Schools, giving demonstrations with pigeons. I had an appointment to visit Ireland for this purpose. That appointment would have taken me to Ireland, and I had arranged with Captain Lockett to go over and return with some friends the following week in the S.S. Leinster.

Agent being dropped by parachute with pigeons and kit.

An urgent call from France necessitated a week's postponement of the appointment, otherwise I should not have been able to write these details.

We crossed the following week and had water-planes and American destroyers to convoy us. Those who made sea trips during the war will have recollections of cork jackets in which they were wrapped, and other discomforts.

I once made a trip on the S.S. Zeelandia, a passenger boat plying between London and Rotterdam throughout the war. On her next voyage she was torpedoed.

On arriving at Harwich, I was put in a pilot cutter and then transferred to a trawler going into the harbour.

When asked to take me on board, the skipper suggested they should chuck me overboard and let me swim. But when on board and he learnt I was O.C. pigeons the greeting was a much more friendly one.

Many pigeons earned fame during the war. The French awarded diplomas in the case of birds deserving the Croix de Guerre or Croix Militaire. When Commandant Raynal was surrounded at Vaux, at times pigeons were his only means of communication with Verdun. His last bird but one flew through a terrible enemy fire, and was awarded the Croix de Guerre. His final pigeon, badly mangled, dropped dead as he delivered his message. He was awarded the Legion d'Honneur, and a diploma framed in the colours of the order hangs at headquarters.

No. 2709 was awarded the V.C. in our own pigeon service, and its mangled remains are to be seen preserved in the United Services Museum. This bird was with our forces fighting at Menin Road, October, 1917. She was despatched with a message from the front line to Divisional Headquarters nine miles away early in the afternoon. She was shot down by the enemy soon after liberation, laid out in the rain all night, but the next morning sufficiently recovered to struggle back with her message, and staggered on the floor of the loft and died before the officer could remove the message-holder from her leg.

"Cher Ami" was the favourite of the American Army, and officers and men of the American C.P.S. are never tired of relating the brave exploits of this little blue chequer. Its photo and that of many other good birds that worked well for the American C.P.S. was sent me. "Cher Ami" delivered no less than twelve important messages on different occasions—never failing. Very often birds were home one day from the trenches with messages and back again the next day so soon as an opportunity occurred to get them back under cover of barrage. "Cher Ami's" last flight was a desperate one on the Argonne, but she bravely got through and delivered her message, although one leg was hanging from the thigh and bleeding profusely. The message was an important one from a Platoon in difficulties. Reinforcements saved the situation, and the men of the Platoon have cause to bless the brave deed of "Cher Ami."

A German loft, with birds and complete equipment, captured at Folies, France, on August 9th, 1918, together with 30 pigeons, was sent to England and exhibited at the Zoological Gardens. The birds kept to the loft and remained there some time. In my opinion the quality of the German pigeons was not equal to those used by our forces.

Mons. Jules with a British pigeon used for Secret Service long flights.

Capt. W. D. Lea Rayner, who succeeded Capt. E. E. Jackson as O.C. Pigeons, Ireland.

Good-bye!—A Naval Pigeon man just sending off a messenger.

Whenever field telegraph or telephone systems were in working order pigeons were not called upon for service. It was only when all other means of communication failed they were used.

For distances up to fifty or sixty miles pigeons were practically infallible. More than 95 per cent. of the messages sent by pigeon post were safely delivered.

During seven months of the year 1916 one military loft in France received no less than twenty-four pigeon messages from aeroplanes which had been captured by the enemy or met with disaster. These messages told the fate of between forty and fifty airmen and their last observations over the enemy lines.

The pigeon service at G.H.Q., Horse Guards, at the start consisted of one officer and a corporal clerk; at the conclusion of the armistice there were four officers, six stationary lofts containing an average of 150 birds in each, and six coastal depots from each of which 300 birds were liberated to fly to the Metropolis almost daily. Corporal MacIntrye, who was with me at the start of the services, remained throughout and proved most efficient in charge of the clerical department, which became an extensive one.

The chief depot at the commencement for the collection of the birds before despatch to the front was 19, Doughty Street, and as the service increased it was necessary to requisition No. 18 as well as 17.

Reinforcements of men and some thousands of birds were retained here.

The birds never saw outside their lofts as squeakers, and with the wire cages on top of the mobile lofts were easily schooled and taught their duties.

The Germans disliked the pigeon service and made several attempts to bomb Doughty Street, on one occasion dropping a bomb in the adjacent garden, doing damage to the depot, but without the loss of a single man or bird.

Major Alec Waley, M.C., had command of the Carrier-Pigeon Service in France.

Captain E. E. Jackson, Captain Gerald Lockett, C. Bryant and Lieut. Jacques served as officers in the organisation of the service and instruction of officers and men for the tanks and other forces.

From the commencement of the war until May, 1916, all pigeon racing was suspended, but on May 1st, 1916, a conference took place at the Home Office at which Lieut.-Col. P. Maud (G.H.Q., Home Forces), Major J. Sealy Clarke (War Office), Assistant Paymaster W. H. Osman (Admiralty), Messrs. A. L. Dixon, C. D. Carew Robinson (Home Office), Mr. A. C. Goodchild (Scottish Office) and Mr. H. A. Tripp took part. At this conference I made out such a strong case that training and restricted racing be allowed, that authority for liberations was subsequently granted. Had this authority been refused for the duration of the war it would, I fear, have been the death blow to our sport instead of its subsequent vigorous renewal and growth. I have given a brief chronological account of the Service, simply detailing facts sufficient, I think, to show that the Carrier-Pigeon Service rendered good and efficient work during the Great War.